The Red Drum

Also by this author

Land & Sea: Poetry Inspired by Art
(2006, 2007)

Unsung Love Songs (2010)

The Lava Storyteller (2013)

The Red Drum
Selected and New Poems

By Cristina M. R. Norcross

Lone Gull Press

Lone Gull Press
Oconomowoc, WI
www.firkinfiction.com
Bookndz@yahoo.com

Manufactured in the United States of America

ISBN-13: 978-1492824992
ISBN-10: 1492824992

ACKNOWLEDGMENTS

I would like to thank my patient and gracious readers
who always welcome a new poem and offer helpful
feedback: Jennifer Peña, Jody Cooper, Michele Wehrwein
Albion, Shannon Jackson Arnold, Rebecca Seymour, Liz
Rhodebeck, Kimberly A. Blanchette, Holly Kallie, Elaine
Silverman Sturm, Darshan Jessop and my husband John
Norcross. Finally, I would like to say thank you to my
parents and my brother for their steadfast faith in all of
my artistic endeavors.

"Acceptance" was published in the 2011 anthology,
Verse & Vision, by the Q Artists Cooperative.

"A Valentine in July" and "Home Fires" also appear in
the book, *Unsung Love Songs* (2010).

"Growing Windows" first appeared in the Spring 2013
issue of Red Cedar.

"Breaking" was featured in the 2011 ARTiculate show,
sponsored by the Bay View Arts Guild.

"Be the Breath" appeared in the September 24, 2013
newsletter issue of Essential Wellness.

For my grandfather, William Raskopf

The Red Drum: List of Poems

The Red Drum

(Inspired by the writing of Stanley Kunitz)

Your heart – a red drum.
Taut leather bound
to the infinite shape of a circle,
seeks the music of other beating hearts.

Sound changes,
when a strong wind blows,
when the leather is rain-soaked,
when the sun makes the circle
jump into the light.

"I made this,"
says the drum.
Dreams take shape in the air,
with each, bellowing note.
"Now change it by living,"
says the drum's stick.
Sing a new song.
"Truth –
Of thee I sing."

Many more layers of change
bring syncopated rhythms,
ballads of longing,
and newly discovered voices.

Your heart is a red drum –
now crimson with passion,
tomorrow the sun makes it pink –
a tender, summer rose.
Sing your transformation to the world.
Beat the drum.
Beat the drum.
Beat the drum.

The Holy Fool's Choice

Enrobed in silk snow –
a blue mountain throne
surrounded by fog
clears to reveal the golden thread
of beauty within.

The trees hold court,
offering up treasures
to the highest peak,
the choicest array of pine needles.
The queen's jewels rest
in the unassuming trunk –
the hidden box.

Only the Holy Fool
knows which head fits the crown.
Beneath the withered tree,
she sleeps.

Rose-colored lenses
paint the sky.
True royalty exists
within thee, Love.
You are the jeweled pendant
set against alabaster skin.

Unfolding

"I am looking for the trail.
Where is my testing-tree?"
~Stanley Kunitz

Darkness speaks of light often,
like an encouraging relative
who vows that big things are coming.

It doesn't last —
the dark cloud,
but then what is forever
in a series of eternal days?

This conscious trespassing
into the nether realm
bears fruit on the page
or canvas.
When the noble mind
surfaces beyond the shadows,
days become luminous.

Wind swept and cared for,
caution carries the wanderer
further down the road
toward the testing-tree.
There is no denying the bark.

Hop scotching from light to dark
brings the chosen path home.
Begin with these steps,
brick-by-brick.
Build the forgotten road —
then walk upon the stars.

Leaving

The camera catches her breath,
her last thought –
the anticipation of tears.
She decides to pack the camera too
after taking a self-portrait.

Maggie never wanted to leave.
The empty bottles
kept gathering though,
like the hopeful at a freedom rally.

She had seen black markings
on his arms before,
but these were fresh.
"Old tattoos," he said.
She knew better.
Maggie was leaving –
tonight.

One leather bag
held no more than she needed,
no less than she wanted
as remembrance –
a brush,
her favorite carnelian stone pendant,
a scarf for the early morning chill
of approaching autumn,
and a Timex watch
that no longer kept time.
She had waited long enough.

With bare wrists
and empty pockets,
Maggie flung her leather satchel
over one shoulder
and shut the door.

We are all lights
burning bright –
under the same, tormented sky.
We are all candles
held at night,
and none of us wear gloves.

I Am the Door

I am the door that will not shut –
a dust cloud
from a shovel of dirt,
cast into the air.
The earth becomes airborne –
no longer a solid form.

A handful of pebbles –
a makeshift memorial
for a boat that used to park here –
now only a rectangle
of dry dust remains.

My child draws a white chalk heart,
scribbling more lines
onto my blue-white journal.

"Stop that, please," I say.
The writing session is over.

"You need a Band Aid, Mommy."

Picking up the Stars

Making peace with the sky –
not knowing where the stars will land,
but picking up every last fragment of fire.

You know me well,
like tea kettles
and leather bound books on a shelf.

I sit often and look for your line -
written on walls,
on street signs,
on the last open door in my mind.

You appear in dreams,
when I do not call you,
rescuing me from some transparent being
and offering a quiet hand
on my warm back.

Our paths cross only once every decade
in prime number years.
Like a puzzle,
we solve each other.
No equations –
only answered prayers.

Acceptance

Branches were cut,
before I could touch
the new, green leaves –
velvet flesh.

I no longer wish for
a brightly colored streamer
to appear,
while I dance into the night.
The air is thick
with choices.

This is time enough.
Rug fibers softened by living,
The carved, wooden legs
of Aunt Mary's side table,
and the chipped place setting
from our wedding,
that didn't quite make it to England.

When I place my finger
on the table by lamplight,
a message in dust appears.
This is the life
you always wanted.
You just don't know it yet.

A Thousand Songs

(Dedicated to the Memory of Edith Piaf)

Large, round eyes send out
disconsolate melodies.
Ringing tones –
pieces of a life
not yet whole.

The Little Sparrow
sings in the streets,
then to an audience,
set out in red velvet rows.
Only songs of the soul
can save this tortured chanteuse
from sparkling lights
and star-studded microphones.

Comfort in dark places
brings light,
when blind eyes,
riddled with illness,
weep.

A thousand songs ring out,
like church bells in unison,
conversing across the courtyard.
Somber hands flutter,
reaching out to touch
"Le Petit Piaf."
Crackled recordings
of voice remain,
conjuring up the presence
of a timeless, majestic bird.

Healing Wounds

Clouds swallow the sun.
Light hidden behind
a blanket of sheer white
and silken swaths of blue,
soften the close of day.

Healing old wounds
can be as gentle as a late summer sunset,
or as blinding as daybreak,
with its unforgiving
unmasking of the day,
forcing eyelids open.
Squinting would be
so much easier.

Confront this self
who still burns with hurt –
still accusing past players
of not following the script.
Forgive yourself first,
then release the memories
of regret and reproach –
ashes and dust dispatched to the sea –
an airborne prayer.

Let the state of no mind prevail.
Do not consult the ego –
he will only encourage
you to spend your soul's currency.
Penny candy and shiny bangles
are temporal entertainment.
Heal old wounds –
then move on.

What We Leave Behind

Trinkets tucked away in a forgotten purse –
offerings wrapped in tiny boxes with cotton –
willed to be worn or stored
by someone else.
We leave this shell –
now clothed in spirit form.

It is all fleeting –
this dream.
The flashes of lightning with wings,
that dance across the green tips of grass
in my backyard,
are neon reminders
of what we see,
what we think we know,
and what we leave behind –
a flash of thought,
inspiration,
a life worth living,
and the remembrance
of light in space.

Shed your skin –
your thin layer of human surface
that only touches the husk of things.
Live brightly –
fully.
Your inner core –
an untumbled gem.

Eulogy of a Poet

The day after I leave,
only sky will remain.
There will be nowhere to sit
at my funeral spread
of cucumber cream cheese triangles
and sweet gerkin pickles,
so people will have to make do
with golden tassled, floating cushions
or tree branches that still refuse to fall.

The birds will gather too,
chattering from the cheap seats.
Standing room only will be occupied by
stray cotton blossoms
in search of the rafters.

Poetry will be read –
some of it mine,
some from my best gal, Emily D.
Words will move about
like liberated particles,
forming a serpent's tail
that rests on shoulders
and curls up on laps
in comfort.

I hope that there is more laughter
than tears –
that people will mingle
and reconnect like puzzles,
each finding a friend to nestle next to,
making genuine promises
of future phone calls.

I hope that when I no longer exist,
my words will remain eternal,
along with my cheeky spirit –
dipping into conversations

and causing a few stammers.
The energy will be bright and fierce,
like the raging ocean of creation.

If I had more time,
I would give the eulogy myself.
Alas, this poem will have to suffice.

A Valentine in July
(For my husband, John)

It is neither snowy nor brisk.
The store windows have
no red hearts
emblazoned on glass.

It is simply time for me
to put my pen and paper away –
to honor your Being
in the same room with me.

It is quiet –
the long day ends.
The slow, dark part of the day
now begins.
You arrive home late
from your plane journey.
The yellow glow of the living room walls
turns to a faint pink wash
from your traveling shadow.

The hallway light is dim.
You sit with jacket still on,
and I watch your mouth,
as you unravel your day before me –
a spray of daisies at my feet.

You are my July Valentine,
as the day's heat becomes softened
by moonlight, and the lazy fan of air conditioning.

The hum of our computers begins again,
but we are joined by thought –
by the evening's gentle air,
and the drops of humidity
on my wine glass.

Luscious Mind

What if I held your hand
and you held mine –
like swans swooning down a river,
only to catch the current,
and glide as one –
for all eternity?

I know your face.
It has creases I have memorized
long ago.
Your eyes soften
when you see my thoughts drift
out the window,
as if you wish to travel
the jagged path of scribbled lists,
and countless wished for endings
in my head.

Where does the writer vanish
when the world stops turning
on its axis –
when the sky breaks open,
like a luscious egg –
the contents of my mind,
a warm, yellow liquid?

It is a bit like Xanadu
all gold, roller-skating muses –
a Pepperland of rainbows and nowhere men,
all playing in the orchestra.

The writer returns triumphant
with words in hand,
images in back pocket,
and a syncopated beat
you can really sing to.

Rising Bubbles

I imagine that I can breathe
inside the glossy bubbles
that I see floating to the surface.
I swim through the water,
eyes wide open,
gazing at the light above.

My limbs push and pull
the water slowly,
as if climbing a mountain sideways.

This is a dream –
moving from one life
to another –
straddling two worlds.
We have only moved states,
but it is a transatlantic shift.

Transitions are steep.
They are thick like molasses –
a reminder that the calm plateau
in between
requires a big push
just to get there.

Chaos eventually allows
for a succinct package of adaptation.
The once dark waters
become more clear –
easier to plunge through
with eager arms and sturdy legs.
Instead of searching for
precious seconds of air from bubbles,
the now acclimated traveler
has gills.

The Sacredness of Now

Waiting for time to elapse –
flipping through a book of film cells,
is never productive.
Like paint drying
or the watched pot,
it cannot be pressured into passing.

Wasted moments –
these periods when you wish
for another heartbeat
to come and save you.
You long for this day to end,
so that the real you
may begin to unfold its wings.

The most beautiful bird in flight
is the one that hangs in the air
with no purpose in mind,
other than eventually calming hunger,
gliding on air
with no effort –
no wing exerting might.

The hawk
can tell you some lies,
if you wish,
about time.
It passes.
It quickens.
It slows to fill space,
in spite of this hurried life.

The only thing worth waiting for –
is for your heart to acknowledge
the sacredness of now.

The Creative Spirit

The creative spirit works in wondrous ways,
bringing hope and heaven
closer to our fingertips.

Flashes of light appear,
like lightning streaks
across the mind's landscape.
A configuration of dots and dashes
dance over the page.
As storm clouds pass,
what remains
are fallen branches –
and this bright, new day.

Only Words

Words scramble down

like ants in succession,

off to war,

in the trenches of melancholy and metaphor.

Only love

can lift us up like doves,

searching for a branch

to make that morning call.

Glorious

(For Jennifer)

Vibrant, deep and glorious.
With an iris spirit,
you create the world,
painting the sky with bold strokes –
adorning the earth with
beaded bangles.

Art in all of its mystery
becomes tangible –
knowable,
when I think of your sight –
your insight.

We stand hand in hand –
souls commingling across thousands of miles,
connected by that invisible,
breathable link,
stringing things that sparkle,
with words that float on the page.

Letters and numbers appear,
and I know that it is your will
sending out a creative code
of breath, gold paint,
and Marilyn's striped top.
Reading and listening for messages,
I hear what you hear.
You see what I see,
and somehow
our canvas is the same.

The orchid and the iris
share hues of blue
and depths of purple
that rage like a flood,
only to dwell in the same waters.

For with a higher purpose
water rises from the ground.

Here, within life's small world,
light appears.
Thank you for being
the shining glow on this stage.

A Cosmic Waltz

A xylophone rings out each note in my head clearly.
The beating in my chest is a steady push.
The humming at my fingertips creates a pattern,
like tiny whirlpools.

This is when I think of us –
our cosmic dance in the universe.
Only we know the choreography.
When I am with you,
the world turns in slow motion.
Cars passing by lose their velocity.

Sometimes we sit on the curb,
knees bent and rigid,
backs curved to aching point.
Our eyes meet in knowledge
of the couple we used to be –
before the little people of our household
started making their impossible demands
and immediate requests.
I jump out of my skin sometimes
from the sheer suddenness of necessity.
My hands have found a parental tremor,
and I wonder if I will ever have a Self again.

But now all is quiet upstairs.
Lullabies have been sung.
Blankets have been tucked.
We have polished the eyelids
of young ones with dreamy promises
and a glimpse of Never Never Land.

If we can move past exhaustion,
let us dance another dance –
in our cosmic world of loving partnership.
Waltz with me now,
before the angels awaken.

Pure Spirit

The body fades to canvas
when you are pure spirit.

You and I are old souls –
amongst older ones
who still haven't learned
their lessons.

Then there are the new souls,
looking for someone to care.
That is why you are here.
Your gifts are too numerous
not to share some light,
some wit,
and wise charms.
Only the charming
can collect an audience,
like butterflies in a cunning net.
The purpose is pure though.

Release –
release them to the day,
so that air may lift up bold orange
wings with black spots –
the spots of a leopard
with cave comforts.

Perhaps, I am a new soul
after all –
seeking answers,
and just one kind word
to get started.

This is the beginning.
We are meant to be a bridge
between this realm and the next.
Do not waiver in your keen sense of duty.

Hold hands in this faltering world.
Open the door.
Here – we'll do it together.

Live Words

Lived out loud
on paper –
inky fingers for show.
A word appears in between black,
swirling thumbprints.

I am just about to catch
the last sloping curve of a "y"
and meaning falls off the page.

Paragraphs are easier
to contain,
to house like square,
squat apartment buildings –
a comma here,
a run on sentence there.
It all becomes code –
a language of lines and enthusiastic dots –
expression with lift off.

Winged words grasp letters
with eager talons,
escaping high into the air
with prized delights.
Words have weight.
They fall to earth,
embedded in dusty text.

Reach in and find a reflection
of who you will become,
if you can bend words
to your will.
You will champion
the hand that writes,
make peace with the higher self
and all the thoughts
that find a home
on lined parchment.

Bring the letters
down from the shelf.
Tame them.
In the corral
a theme will appear.

You will materialize
in the story you write.
You will rise to the inky surface.

Hide and Seek

(Dedicated to Virginia Woolf)

Hidden in carefully chosen words
are the rough crevices of hard times –
the pitfalls of selfhood.

You listen to my anguish,
my parallel drop,
like a graph charting stock market losses.
I relive the minute scratches,
as if there is no way to smooth over
or polish the marks I have made,
on your soul and mine.

Hard times –
we are all having them,
but your road is the hardest, you think.
Yours is the damp cloth, that will not dry.
Mine too –
see how much we have in common?

I keep pace with your steps,
and the light in the corner of your eyes
shows that there are many
years and miles for us to walk.
Your road has chunks of gravel,
while mine has debris
that will not be tidied.

Come home soon.
I will try to be there too.
Departures occur too often
for my pockets to allow.
I walk into waters
with Her heavy weight,
but she has paved the way with words.
I may just borrow a few.

In This Town

(A tribute to every small town in America)

The streets have gaps like missing teeth.
Cars drop with a thud into muddy water and gravel.
It's a miracle that a ten minute trip
takes you to another part of town.

The shoe store is vacant where it once thrived,
with metal measuring instruments
and balloons for smiling faces
with tiny feet.

A coffee shop shines in the center
where you can linger over a cup,
where a chess set is always left out,
and a carved plaque reads:
"Every misfortune is merely an opportunity in disguise".

This is where life in old brick buildings
carries on.
No personal complaint could ever compare
to some far worse tragedy.
These are people who survive –
cheerfully.

In the winter,
the snow falls like a curtain.
Residents hibernate inside
until the roads are cleared,
then ski on the clean, white blankets,
surrounded by sunshine.

In the summer,
festivals visit
and families come together
to greet the long day
with community barbecues.
At night, when the air is still warm
and babies sleep on capable shoulders,

the drive-in theater plays a show
to the night sky.

In this town
you are welcome
to join the life that exists,
the life that carries on
from the past.
The old and the new live
in parallel –
in the buildings, in the people,
and in the lakes
that reflect the harmony
of this town.

Bones

Mouth wide open,
catching the mist
that falls on white bones and teeth
with fog for camouflage.

These are the remains –
huddled, protected by the side of our house.
It is a deer left behind
from many seasons ago
and collected by the former homeowner –
a relic of wildlife.

I am unnerved by the skeleton's presence,
and yet for months
I cannot bring myself to remove it,
for fear of disturbing
nature's memorial.

At the first sign of interest
from eager, little hands,
I spirit away the bones
without a thought.
Perhaps this is the best way –
to replace care for the living
where only teeth in a hollow form existed.
The deer would have wanted it that way.

Bones are like words –
all angles and distinctness,
yet meaning and marrow
are more porous.
These bone-like words are my tribute
to what nature leaves behind,
and what nature takes back,
to be renewed, reconstituted
into the lives of many more
who will roam this marshy land.

No Progress

Sitting with eyes closed,
I try not to crowd the empty space
with thought.
The world rushes in –
images, sensations,
insistent memories.

I start afresh,
rejecting the mind's interruption
by counting to ten
in deep concentration.
Impatient, my mind sends another visitor
to disturb this quiet meditation.

The key is to have no goal in mind –
no achievement,
no record of progress.
Sitting in silence invites the divine within,
if you can manage to keep
the psyche's many voices at bay.

A new guide appears –
Maori, I think,
or, Native American.
"You are not really here," he says.
"This thought that you are solid,
experiencing pain,
this is what is holding you back.
Remember your spiritual home,
and its image will never leave your heart again.

We all celebrate life on earth
in a unique way.
Embrace *your* celebration
and be
here.

Tipping the Moon

We are tipping the moon until daybreak –
moving the crescent
until there is no darkness in the sky,
only a salmon pink –
the earliest light of day.

As I look out the window with my son,
there is a fire,
just above the line of trees across the street.
Every time I blink,
the color seems to rise.
There is no escaping the constant changes
of pigmentation and light.

An out-of-date photograph of a child
sits proudly on the mantelpiece,
next to old postcards and holiday greetings.
It is a moment captured,
but never to be repeated.
Like the sunrise refusing to halt,
time keeps adding another year
to the child's age.

Scenes of life blend together,
moving fast to the echoed melody of a carousel.
I am left with the glowing embers of another day,
and time to appreciate the moon.

Every day we move.
Every day we are tipping the moon.

Fresh

The red marking of a sand hill crane appears,
moving across the back lawn
in subtle, determined movements.
Each of the four, golden-feathered birds
is a brilliant sight
of family and winged worth.

Awestruck, we stand with noses against the glass,
seeing our bird family doppelganger
glide across the grass
in search of food –
a humble group.

Inside we rearrange the refrigerator,
looking for sustenance
that requires little actual cooking.
The cranes are also seeking a shared meal.
They seem much calmer than we,
in our flustered search,
as if we haven't eaten in months.

There is much to admire in the slow, steady
approach of nature.
Always assured that the environment will provide.
Always content with what is found.

To have that kind of faith in provisions
and satisfaction with what is –
this is what humans lack,
with our misty fresh vegetables
and plastic container clad deli counters.

Nature is simply –
as fresh as it gets.

Medicine Buddha of Azure Blue

His body is azure blue –
his skin as cold as polar ice.
With warm eyes,
a fire is lit from behind oval shapes,
offering a healing hand
and strong shoulders,
with sloping curves.
His crossed knees are restful plateaus.

A carnival of life
surrounds his serene pedestal.
This confusion on the periphery
does not draw him away
from the peaceful center he holds
in the stillness of his palm.

We look for this restful pause in our lives,
only to find a constant movement
of our brains –
a fluttering of hopping thoughts
and scurrying plans to be busy.
We should stop
and simply – be.
This is when the medicine melts
into the psyche,
and soothes the weary brow of the
Western soul.

His body is azure blue,
and I am too busy looking
for other colors.
His shoulders are enrobed in fire,
like honey pots in summer.
I see his vision for the first time,
and it teaches me to see my thirst
as a useful hunger.

Home Fires

Coming home,
you bring with you
traces of travel –
the scent of rushing to the latest gate change,
the sound of tired baggage
landing on a black conveyor belt.

Greeted by high pitched screams
and tiny feet running on the hardwood floor,
elation fills the air
with one simple word –
"Daddy!"

Our two sons rush to give you
a group hug,
one they've been waiting for
for days,
as you plant a gentle kiss on my cheek
and convey a look that asks hesitantly,
"How was your week?"

Our patterns of splashy baths,
trips to the park,
endless laundry, dishes,
meals and snacks to prepare in succession,
urgent trips to the potty
and sweet stories and whisperings
before bedtime
measure time for us –
we who keep the home fires burning.

We are in essence keeping time.
Our week has high points of play
and soft, happy moments of affection.
It also has chaotic, circus-like moments
of cleaning up sticky messes and refereeing squabbles,
that leaves me wanting to pull my hair out.

We are keeping time though,
until you come home
and make our grouping of three
a family of four again.

"There is more to life than
just getting through the week," you say.
But this is my pattern –
my home fire.
This is what I know.

Second Glance

I am the guardian
of butterfly souls.
It is my second rescue
in under a year.
This orange beauty was opening
and closing its wings,
quite dangerously,
on a highway ramp.
I saw the flash of black and gold
and tried to stop,
realizing that I was too far off.

I saw a diagonal thread of golden light
jump into my line of vision.
I knew that I had to find my way back
to this winged friend.
At the next opening,
I turned around
and found my way back to fate's corner.
The butterfly was still struggling,
so I watched for traffic,
as I gently lifted him onto my palm,
leaping back to the safety
of the grass covered edge.
Finding a circle of clearing amongst the green,
I noticed that one wing was torn,
giving reason for interrupted flight.

I am dreaming of renewed lift off,
as this butterfly alights into the blue.
Perhaps he won't survive the tear.
We will see if that flash of light returns
to say that all is well.
Little lines in the shape of healed wings
will give hope
for the rest –
all creatures of light –
all searching for the safety
of home.

Sit

A straight-backed chair supports
what posture ought to be.
A plush, blue velvet cushion
with patterned crests –
provides a curved, hollow
when guests sit to rest.

I imagine ancestors taking turns in this chair.
Their presences alternating –
changing the energy patterns
of the room.

Sit …
you have nowhere urgent to go right now.
Sit …
it is only a clock
with revolving numbers
like a turnstile.

Sit with yourself,
for the first time,
and ask no questions.
Do not scribble found thoughts.
Just sit
and observe the self.

A ceramic square,
missing its hot teapot,
informs me,
"You are the apple of God's eye."

...rrow

...could be a field of tomorrows,
...pulated by an expanse of red poppies,
heralding the dawn.

But, this tomorrow I wish for
exists beyond my reach,
so I will hope that the day after that is a good day.
It will be a day that I will exist in forever –
this paradise we speak of –
this home we return to when God's loving embrace
is the only garment our spirits wear.

Winter Light in Portland

A pale blue light beckons me
across the bridge.
Cool air whispers, like a lover whose hand
cannot leave mine.
In this winter light,
a secret garden exists in Portland.

Snow covers every branch –
every liquid, white surface.
Clustered crystals cover my ears,
so that cars in the distance cease to exist.

I am a winter garden guest.
The bridge has no footsteps,
except for future outlines of my departure.

Like a snow globe untouched,
this world of stillness and reflected light
gently holds my fate.
Waking from a dream could not be as tender
as my garden companion.

Imprinted with droplets
from a melting snowflake,
my hands will never be the same.
My feet glide over the bridge,
and I memorize this sacred place,
like a photograph,
where I once did dwell
for an afternoon in Portland.

Your Heart is the World

(Inspired by the heart-centered writing of Ingrid Goff-Maidoff)

Your heart is love.
It has only ever known LOVE.
Bring to your life
the pureness of this emotion.
Break through the stones
created by man,
with stacked regimentation
and then disperse it,
like you are spreading the Word.

Use abandonment and freedom
that only angels' hands
know the texture of –
that only a good listener can touch.

Your heart is the world.
You are a wellspring of love.
Feel it in your bones,
the way the earth feels
the tender soles of your feet
with each step.
Feel this love.

Your heart is the world –
The world is your heart.

Your Red Ribbon

This is your red ribbon –
your crooked river to the other side of now.
It ties a bright reminder
on the end of your finger.
You lift your head and see,
as if for the first time,
the breath a dove takes
before its solitary song.
You lift your chin –
a proud face –
as you walk into the world
once again.

Like a Button

A black, round button wants for nothing.
It has only plastic aspirations
to be threaded –
wedded to the velvet jacket
like the other, useful buttons –
striving only to serve.
Be more like the button.

Growing Windows

What the body remembers
is the swell of oceans –
the tumult of lengthening limbs –
hands that start writing
the stories of age
with each stretching muscle.

No bump is showing –
yet I'm feeling thick around the middle.
My soft, tender belly
knows curves –
roundness was here for three pregnancies.
Two of them stayed and grew.

A woman's torso extends to fill space.
Age walks –
it wanders into wisdom unknowingly
and finds the longest book to read.
We may be here awhile,
says the body.
Take root,
grow windows
and look out.

, A Meditation

ind
to play –
touch to every inch of skin.
ound reverberates
and rei̇̇es, mind and muscles,
because you are exactly where you need to be.

You are the pearl with glowing curves
rolling toward an open hand.
Every length and depth of you is beautiful –
from the rising of your shoulders in sleep
to the tender arch of your foot,
held with care by softened leather.

Your divine purpose reaches across every golden field
and every pebbled road to meet the beginning of you.
For you are the world,
and the world exists in you –
in beauty and in acceptance.

Behold, you are the sheen and honeyed glow of your skin.
Know that you are this fullness –
this rich delight.
Whole and healed –
you are the gift.

Breaking

We break apart –
revelation –
the inside shards and hollow of a geode.

Surfaces melt away.
Take no cover –
these red curves spill.
We are One Being –
you, me, he, she.

Kaleidoscopic difference
lights the way.
Underneath –
the solid core of what we hold dear.
We rip away the old –
peeling precious debris –
touching something real.
We are breaking.

Author Biography

Cristina M. R. Norcross is the author of *Land & Sea: Poetry inspired by Art* (2006, 2007), *The Red Drum* (2008, 2013), *Unsung Love Songs* (2010) and *The Lava Storyteller* (2013). Her works appear in North American and international journals, such as, The Toronto Quarterly, Red Cedar, The Nervous Breakdown and Your Daily Poem. Featured in the BVAG show ARTiculate (2011, 2012), Cristina's work also appears in the anthologies, *Contemporary Women's Literature* (2007), *Verse & Vision* (2011, 2012) and *Sounds of Solace* (forthcoming). She was the co-editor for the project *One Vision: a Fusion of Art and Poetry in Lake Country* (2009-11) and is currently one of the co-organizers of Random Acts of Poetry and Art Day. To find out more, visit: www.firkinfiction.com.